HORRID HENRY'S

Annual 2008

Francesca Simon

Illustrated by Tony Ross

Orion
Children's Books

First published in Great Britain in 2007
by Orion Children's Books
a division of the Orion Publishing Group Ltd
Orion House
5 Upper Saint Martin's Lane
London WC2H 9EA

An Hachette Livre UK Company

1 3 5 7 9 10 8 6 4 2

Horrid Henry's Annual 2008 © Orion Children's Books 2007
Compiled by Sally Byford from the *Horrid Henry* books
by Francesca Simon, illustrated by Tony Ross
Illustrations © Tony Ross 2007
TV animation images © Novel Entertainment Limited 2007
Designed by Dave Unwin, Benedict Lewis and Andy Mcpherson

The Orion Publishing Group's policy is to use papers that are natural,
renewable and recyclable products and made from wood grown in sustainable forests.
The logging and manufacturing processes are expected to conform to the
environmental regulations of the country of origin.

ISBN 978 1 84255 625 2

A catalogue record for this book is available from the British Library

Printed in Italy

www.orionbooks.co.uk
www.horridhenry.co.uk
www.citv.co.uk

Contents

Hello from Horrid Henry   9

New Year's Resolutions   10

How to Make a Horrid Hanger   12

Fun Fact Files: Back to School   14

Bring Horrid Henry and his Classmates to Life   16

Who's Your Best Friend?   18

Horrid Henry's Bedtime   20

Dad's Perfect Pancakes   33

What's Your Perfect Party?   34

How to Make a Valentine's Card - Horrid Henry Style!   36

Spring Sudokus   38

Mother's Day   39

Easter Egg Hunt   40

Are You an Egg Head?   42

Fun Fact Files: Foes   44

Horrid Henry's Perfect Pranks   45

How to Make a Funny Fortune-Teller   46

Passover Puzzle   47

Pet Fact Files   48

Fun Fact Files: Friends   49

Horrid Henry's Homework   50

Father's Day   52

Creepy-Crawly Pizza   53

Horrid Henry's School Fair   54

Cross Country Run   56

Miss Battle-Axe's School Report   57

Horrid Henry's Top Parent-Taming Tips   58

Horrid Henry Goes Global   59

Write Your Own Horrid Henry Story   60

How to Run a Club   62

Club Rules   64

Make a Wicked Waterbomb   65

Secret Messages   66

Horrid Henry's Diary   68

Horrid Henry's Hike   72

Halloween Happenings   74

Horrid Henry's Halloween Feel Box   76

Sparkling Dot-to-Dot   77

Christmas Criss-Cross   78

Horrid Henry's Christmas Presents   79

Christmas Crackers   80

Horrid Henry's Top Ten Triumphs of the Year   82

Horrid Henry's Last Word   83

Puzzle Answers   84

Hello Everyone,

Yippee! This mega-mean annual is all about ME. Find out Fun Facts about me and my friends, see what I get up to all year, and discover some really useful stuff, like my top Parent-Taming Tips.

If your parents are stinky, like mine, and ban you from watching TV, check out all the other things you can do, like puzzles and quizzes and making things out of scraps of paper and lots of gloppy glue – SPLAT!

Have fun!

Henry

What do you call a girl with a frog on her head?

Lily

New Year's Resolutions

My New Years Resolutions

to eat lots of sweets
to make lots of money
to do **NO** homework

to watch 16 hours of T.V. a day
— Whoopee !!!

to become King Henry the Horrible
and rool the World
Henry

My New Year's Resolutions

to eat 5 portions of fruit and
vegetables every day

to be nice to Henry, even though
he's horrible to me

to keep my bedroom tidy at
all times

to do a good deed every day

to help Mum and dad with
the housework

Peter. X

My New Year's Resolutions

to eat 5 portions of fruit and
vegetables every day and give all
my sweets and cakes and biskits to
Henry
to be nice to Henry, even though
he's horrible to me because
so nice

to keep my bedroom tidy at
all times and keep out
of Henry's room
to do a good deed every day by giving
Henry all my pocket
money.
to help Mum and dad with
the housework and do all
Henry's chores for him
Peter. X

What are your New Year's Resolutions?
Write them down here.

11

How to make a Horrid Hanger

Henry puts a horrible hanger on his bedroom door to scare Perfect Peter away. Follow the instructions and see if you can make your door hanger as scary as Horrid Henry's.

You will need:

Cardboard or paper
Glue (if you are using paper)
Tracing paper
Scissors
Pencils, pens or paints

Instructions:

1. Copy or trace the template onto your cardboard or paper and cut out the door hanger.

   If you're using paper, cut out two copies of the template and glue them together. This will make your door hanger stronger. But don't do any writing or decoration until the glue is dry.

2. Write a message on your door hanger. You can put a different message on each side, for example:

   Side 1: ENTER AT YOUR PERIL! or PRIVATE! KEEP OUT!

   Side 2: WELCOME! or PLEASE COME IN!

   Remember to turn your door hanger to the correct side or you might frighten away your friends.

3. If you like, you can decorate your door hanger with pictures or patterns.

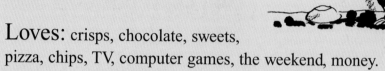

HORRID HENRY

Loves: crisps, chocolate, sweets, pizza, chips, TV, computer games, the weekend, money.

Hates: Moody Margaret, Perfect Peter, Stuck-Up Steve, Bossy Bill, school dinners, vegetables, getting out of bed, bedtime, injections.

Best Friend: Rude Ralph.

WHEN I GROW UP I WANT TO BE:
King Henry the Horrible and rule the world.

MOODY MARGARET

Loves: being the boss.

Hates: Horrid Henry and anyone who doesn't do what I tell them.

Best Friend: Sour Susan – but only when she does what she is told.

WHEN I GROW UP I WANT TO BE:
Prime Minister.

SOUR SUSAN

Loves: telling tales.

Hates: being told what to do.

Best Friend: Moody Margaret, when she isn't being a horrible moody old bossyboots grouch.

WHEN I GROW UP I WANT TO BE: a gossip columnist.

RUDE RALPH

Loves: burping.

Hates: saying 'please', 'thank you', 'sorry' and 'you're welcome'.

Best Friend: Horrid Henry, 'cause he's rude, too.

WHEN I GROW UP I WANT TO BE: rude all the time.

Bring Horrid Henry and his Classmates to Life

You will need:

Cardboard
Tracing Paper
Scissors
Pencils, pens or paints

Instructions:

1. Trace or copy a character onto your cardboard.
2. Colour it in.
3. Carefully cut it out.
4. Cut along the dotted line, as shown on the template.
5. Make a base for your character by tracing or copying the base template onto your cardboard and cutting it out. Cut along the dotted line, and slot your character onto the base.

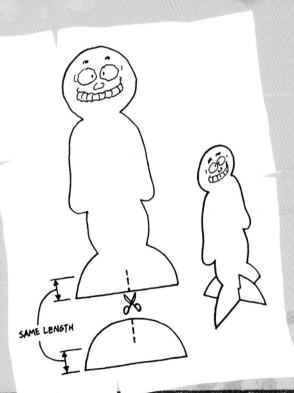

SAME LENGTH

base

Who's your Best Friend?

Horrid Henry and Rude Ralph are best friends because they're both rude and horrid. Try this quiz and find out which of Henry's classmates would be your best friend.

What do you like best about school?

(a) Lessons, especially science and maths.
(b) Painting and drawing, and putting on plays, so I can wear beautiful costumes.
(c) Playtime, so I can sneak loads of sweets.

What kind of games do you like best?

(a) General knowledge quizzes – I always get the answers right.
(b) Dressing up games.
(c) Computer games, like Intergalactic Killer Robots.

What makes you laugh?

(a) Witty, well-written books.
(b) Somebody being silly in class gives me the giggles.
(c) Anyone who burps or farts, especially a teacher!

How do you like to dress?

(a) I like bright, loud clothes – I might be very clever, but I can still look good.
(b) I like pretty, flowing clothes, decorated with flowers or butterflies.
(c) I don't care, as long as I've got cool trainers.

Describe your perfect day . . .

(a) I'd visit an interesting museum, do lots of challenging maths homework, then relax with a book of facts and watch a documentary on TV.

(b) I'd spend all day shopping and buy lots of new clothes, then get dressed up and go to a pampering party with my friends.

(c) I'd watch TV and eat crisps, play computer games – and never ever go to bed!

Answers

Mostly (a)s:

Your ideal best friend is Brainy Brian. Like him, you enjoy doing lots of hard homework, and are so busy being clever that you haven't much time for fun and games. But you do like to dress in bright clothes, so there's definitely a fun-loving side to your personality waiting to burst out.

Mostly (b)s:

Your ideal best friend is Gorgeous Gurinder. Like her, you love dressing up in pretty clothes, giggling with your friends and going to parties. And with your love of beautiful things, you're probably also very good at art.

Mostly (c)s:

Uh oh! Just like Rude Ralph, your ideal best friend is Horrid Henry. There's nothing you like more than annoying people, especially teachers and parents. When you're not being rude and horrid, you're probably asleep!

A HORRID HENRY STORY
Horrid Henry's Bedtime

'What are you doing in my room?' screamed Horrid Henry.

How dare Peter come into his bedroom? Couldn't he read the sign?

'Looking for my blue pencil,' said Peter. He stared at the piles of comics and sweet wrappers and dirty clothes and toys littering the floor, the bed and the chest of drawers.

'Well it's not in here, so get out,' hissed Henry. So what if he'd pinched Peter's pencil? He'd had a huge bit of sky to colour in. 'And don't you dare touch anything.'

'You should be in your pyjamas,' said Perfect Peter. '*I* am.'

'**WHOOPEE FOR YOU**,' said Horrid Henry. 'Now get lost.'

Peter wrinkled his nose. 'Your room stinks.'

'That's 'cause you're in it, smelly.'

'Mum!' screamed Peter. 'Henry called me smelly.'

'Stop being horrid, Henry!' screamed Mum.

'Smelly, smelly, smelly,' jeered Henry. 'Smelly, smelly, smelly.'

'MUM!' wailed Peter. 'He did it again.'

'Tattle-tale!'

'Meanie!'

'Poo breath!'

'Stinky!'

'Mega-stink!'

Perfect Peter paused. He'd run out of bad names to call Henry.

Horrid Henry had not run out of bad names to call Peter.

'Baby! Nappy-Face! Ugg! Worm! Toad! Ugly! Pongy-Pants! Duke of Poop!'

'MUUUUMMMMM!' screamed Peter.

Mum and Dad burst into the room.

'That's enough!' shouted Mum. She looked at her watch. 'It's eight o'clock. Why aren't you in your pyjamas, Henry? Bedtime, both of you.'

'Hurray,' said Perfect Peter. 'I love going to bed.'

What? Bedtime?

The hateful, horrible word thudded round the room.

'NO!' shrieked Horrid Henry. It couldn't be bedtime *already*.

'I'm sorry I've been naughty, Mum,' said Perfect Peter. 'I was so busy doing tomorrow night's homework I didn't notice the time.'

'Don't worry,' said Mum, smiling.

Then she scowled at Henry.

'Why aren't you ready for bed? Peter is.'

'I'm not tired!' screamed Henry. 'I don't want to go to bed.'

'I do,' said Perfect Peter.

Mum sighed.

21

Dad sighed.

'Henry, you know the rules,' said Dad. 'In bed at eight. Lights out at eight-thirty.'

'It's not fair!' screamed Henry. 'No one goes to bed at eight.' Except for Lazy Linda, who was asleep at seven, no one went to bed so early. Toby went to bed at nine. Margaret went to bed at nine-thirty (so she said, though Henry wasn't sure he believed her). Ralph didn't even have a bedtime.

But no. His mean, horrible parents hated him so much they shoved him into bed when everyone else was still rampaging and having fun.

Bedtime. Bleeech. What a hateful, horrible, evil word. A word, thought Horrid Henry bitterly, as horrid as *cabbage*, *prison*, *Peter*, and *school*. When he was King any parent who dared to tell their kids to go to bed would be sent to bed themselves at five o'clock forever.

AAARRGGHH! Why did he have to go to bed? He had TV to watch! Computer games to play! Comics to read!

'But I'm not tired!' howled Henry.

'We're growing boys, Henry, and we need our rest,' said Perfect Peter. 'Early to bed, early to rise, makes a boy healthy, wealthy—'

'Shut up, Peter,' snarled Henry, pouncing. He was Hurricane Henry, blowing away the last remaining human.

'AIEEEEEEE!' screeched Peter.

'Stop being horrid, Henry!' yelled Mum.

'Go to bed this minute!' yelled Dad.

'NO!' shouted Henry.

'Yes!' shouted Mum.

His parents didn't have a bedtime. Oh no. They could stay up as late as they liked. It was so unfair.

'I'm not tired and I won't go to bed!' shrieked Henry. He lay on the floor, kicking and screaming.

Mum looked at Dad.

Dad looked at Mum.

'My turn to put Peter to bed,' shouted Dad, trying to be heard over Henry's howls.

'*My* turn to put Peter to bed,' shouted Mum. 'I got Henry into bed last night.'

'Uhh uhh . . . are you sure?' screeched Dad. He looked pale.

'YES!' shouted Mum. 'How could I forget? Come on, Peter, what do you want for your bedtime story?'

'*Sammy the Snuggly Snail*,' said Perfect Peter, scampering off to bed. '*Slimy the Slug* was too scary.'

Mum scampered after him.

'I WON'T GO TO BED! I want to watch *Cannibal Cook*!' howled Henry.

Cannibal Cook was this brilliant new TV show where chefs competed to see who could cook the most revolting meals. Last time *Gourmet Greg* had whipped up lizard eyes in custard. Tonight *Nibbling Nigel* was fighting back with jellied worm soufflé.

'It's so *boring* being in bed,' screamed Henry.

'I don't care,' said Dad firmly. 'It's bedtime – now!'

Strange, thought Horrid Henry as he paused for breath between shrieks. At night, he never wanted to get into bed, but in the morning he never wanted to get out of it.

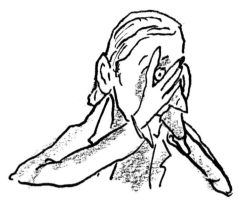

But now was not the time for philosophy. He had important work to do if he was going to delay the evil moment as long as he possibly could.

'Just let me finish my drawing.'

'No,' said Dad.

'Please.'

'N-o spells no,' said Dad.

'It's my homework,' lied Henry.

'Oh all right,' said Dad. 'Hurry up.'

Henry drew a dragon very slowly.

Dad looked at the clock. It was 8:35.

'Come on, Henry,' said Dad. He stood there tapping his foot.

Henry coloured in the dragon very very slowly.

'Henry . . .' said Dad.

Henry drew the dragon's cave very very very slowly.

'That's enough, Henry,' said Dad. 'Now get into your pyjamas and brush your teeth and get into bed.'

'I've already brushed my teeth,' said Henry.

'Henry . . .' said Dad.

'Oh all right,' said Horrid Henry. After all, he held the record for the world's slowest tooth brusher.

Slowly Henry brushed his front teeth. Slowly Henry brushed his back teeth.

Brush.
Brush.
Brush.
Brush.
Brush.

Dad stood in the doorway glaring.

'Hurry up!'

'But Dad,' said Horrid Henry indignantly. 'Do you want me to get fillings?'

'Bed. Now.'

'You'll be sorry when my teeth all fall out because you stopped me from brushing them,' said Henry.

Dad sighed. He'd been sighing a lot lately.

'I can't walk – I'm too floppy,' said Horrid Henry.

'So crawl,' said Dad.

'My legs are too wobbly,' moaned Horrid Henry.

'So wobble,' said Dad.

Delicious smells floated up from the kitchen. Mum was cooking spaghetti with meatballs. Only his favourite dinner. How could he be expected to go to bed with all that good cooking going on downstairs?

'I'm hungry,' said Henry.

'The kitchen is closed,' said Dad.

'I'm thirsty,' said Henry.

'I'll bring you water once you're in bed.'

Dad was being tough tonight, thought Horrid Henry. But not too tough for me.

And then suddenly Horrid Henry had an idea. A brilliant, spectacular idea. True, his parents could make him go to bed – eventually. But they couldn't make him *stay* there, could they?

Horrid Henry yawned loudly.

'I guess I am quite tired, Dad,' said Horrid Henry. 'Will you tuck me in?'

'I said, get into – what did you say?'

'I'm ready for bed now,' said Henry.

Horrid Henry walked to his bedroom and jumped into bed.

'Goodnight Dad,' said Henry.

'Goodnight Henry,' said Dad, tucking him in. 'Sleep well,' he added, leaving the room with a big, beaming smile on his face.

Horrid Henry leapt out of bed. Quickly he gathered up some blankets and a pile of dirty clothes from the floor.

Then he stuffed blanket and clothes under the duvet. Perfect, thought Horrid Henry. Anyone glancing in would think he was snuggled up in bed fast asleep under the covers.

Tee hee, thought Horrid Henry.

He tiptoed to the door.

The coast was clear. His parents were safely in the kitchen eating dinner, leaving Henry a whole house to have fun in.

Sneak Sneak Sneak

Then suddenly Henry heard his parents' voices. Yikes! They were coming upstairs. Henry darted back into his bedroom and hid behind the door.

'He's in *bed*?' said Mum incredulously. 'Before nine o'clock?'

'Yup,' said Dad.

'This I have to see,' said Mum.

His parents stood outside his bedroom peeking in.

'See?' whispered Dad proudly. 'I told you, you just have to be firm.'

Mum marched over to Henry's bed and pulled back the duvet.

'Oh,' said Dad.

Horrid Henry slipped out of his room and dashed downstairs. There was only one thing to do. Hide!

'HENRY!' bellowed Dad, running down the hall. 'Where are you? Get back in bed this minute!'

Horrid Henry squeezed under the sitting room sofa. They couldn't make him go back to bed if they couldn't *find* him, could they?

'Have you found Henry yet?' he heard Dad call Mum.

'No,' said Mum.

Tee hee, thought Horrid Henry.

'Is he in the loo?' said Mum.

'No,' said Dad.

'The kitchen?'

'No,' said Dad.

'Maybe he's gone to bed,' said Mum. She sounded doubtful.

'Fat chance,' said Dad.

Henry heard Mum and Dad's footsteps coming into the sitting room. He held his breath.

'Henry . . .' said Dad. 'We know you're in here. Come out this minute or you're in big trouble.'

Henry kept as still as he could.

Mum checked behind the sofa.

Dad checked behind the TV.

Hmmn.

'I'll check Peter's room,' said Mum.

'I'll check Henry's room again,' said Dad.

The moment they left the room, Henry leapt out and dashed to the coat cupboard in the hall. They'd never find him here.

Henry made himself comfy and cosy in the corner with the wellies. Ahh, this was the life! He'd be safe here for hours. Days. Weeks. When the coast was clear he'd sneak out for food and comics. No more school. No more bed. He'd never leave his little hidey hole until he was grown up and could stay up forever.

Uh oh. Footsteps.

Henry jumped up and dangled from the coat rail, hiding himself as best he could behind the coats.

Dad flung open the cupboard door.

Horrid Henry hung on to the coat rail. His feet dangled.

Please don't find me, thought Henry. Please, please don't find me.

Dad pawed through the coats.

Horrid Henry held his breath.

He hung on tighter and tighter . . .

Dad closed the door.

Phew, thought Henry. That was close.

CR—ACK!
CRASH!

Coats, rail and Henry collapsed to the floor.

'Hi Dad,' said Horrid Henry.

'What are you doing here?'

All was not lost, thought Horrid Henry as he lay in his boring bed with the lights off. His mean, horrible parents could make him go to bed, but they couldn't make him sleep, could they? Ha ha ha. He'd been *pretending* to be asleep. Now that the coast was clear – party!

Henry took his torch, a big stash of comic books, sweets, toys, his cassette player and a few Driller Cannibal tapes and made a secret den under his duvet.

Now, this was more like it.

'Tear down the school! Don't be a fool!' warbled the Driller Cannibals. 'Watcha waitin' for?'

'Ahh, don't be a fool!' sang Henry, stuffing his face with sweets.

'What's going on in here?' screamed Dad, flinging back the duvet.

Rats, thought Henry.

Dad confiscated his flashlight, food, comics and tapes.

'It's eleven o'clock,' said Dad through gritted teeth. 'Go to sleep.'

Horrid Henry lay quietly for thirty seconds.

'I can't sleep!' shouted Henry.

'Try!' screamed Mum.

'I can't,' said Henry.

'Think lovely thoughts,' said Dad.

Horrid Henry thought about monsters.
Horrid Henry thought about ghosts.
Horrid Henry thought about burglars.
Horrid Henry thought about injections . .

'DAD!'

'What?'

'The hall light isn't on.'

Dad plodded up the stairs and turned it on.

'Dad!'

'WHAT?'

'My door's not open enough.'

Dad trudged up the stairs and opened it.

'Dad!'

'What?' whimpered Dad.

'Where's Mr Kill? You know I can't sleep without Mr Kill.'

'I'll look for him,' said Dad, yawning.

'And I need to be tucked in again,' said Henry.

Dad left the room.

Horrid Henry was outraged. Humph, wasn't that just like a parent? They nag and nag you to go to bed and when you tell them you're ready to sleep, suddenly they don't want to know.

Henry waited. And waited. And waited.

The clock said 11:42.

Still no Dad. And no Mr Kill.

'Dad?'

There was no answer.

'Dad!' hissed Henry.

Still there was no answer.

Henry jumped out of bed. Where was Dad? He needed to be tucked in. How could they expect him to sleep without being tucked in?

Henry peeped into the hall.

No Dad.

Henry checked the bathroom.

No Dad.

He walked downstairs and checked the kitchen.

Still no Dad.

What a rotten father, thought Horrid Henry. To abandon his son without tucking him in . . .

Henry peeked into the sitting room.

'Dad?'

Dad was lying on the sofa holding Mr Kill and snoring.

'Hey Dad, wake up!' shrieked Horrid Henry. 'I'm ready for bed now!'

THE END

Dad's Perfect Pancakes

It's Pancake Day and Horrid Henry's dad is busy in the kitchen. Here's his recipe for perfect pancakes. Ask a grown-up to cook them with you. If you're lucky they might let you toss one. Try to catch it in the pan!

You will need:

100g (4oz) plain flour
1 large egg
300ml (1/2 pint) milk
Pinch of salt
50g (2oz) butter

Instructions:

(makes about 10 pancakes):

1. Sift the flour and pinch of salt into a large mixing bowl and make a well in the middle.

2. Break the egg into the well. Using a fork or a whisk, beat the egg, mixing in the flour gradually from around the sides.

3. Add in the milk a little at a time, and beat the mixture until it is smooth.

4. Heat a little butter in a frying pan until it's very hot.

5. Pour about 2-3 tablespoons of the batter into the pan.

6. Quickly tilt the pan so that the batter covers the base of the pan.

7. Cook on a medium heat for about 1 minute, until the pancake is golden.

8. Flip the pancake and cook for 1 minute on the other side too.

9. Delicious with lemon juice and sugar, or lashings of maple syrup!

Horrid Henry is also in the kitchen making GLOP.

In goes:

One sprinkling of porridge oats
One dollop of coleslaw
One spoonful of coffee
Some yoghurt
Two teaspoons of vinegar
Some old baked beans
One spoonful of mustard
One squirt of ketchup
…or whatever he can find in the kitchen.

He throws all the ingredients into the mixer. Then turns it on very fast. Yuck, Henry! Whatever you do – don't eat it!

What's your Perfect Party?

Horrid Henry's birthday is in February, his favourite month. He longs for a party at Lazer Zap. What's your dream party?

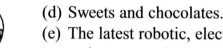

Where would you like to have your party?

(a) At home, with my parents watching to make sure that nobody's horrid.
(b) Outdoors, so there's lots of space to run around.
(c) In my bedroom, surrounded by all my new presents.
(d) At a restaurant with top nosh.
(e) Somewhere with lots of dark tunnels.

Who would you like to invite?

(a) No more than five or six nice, well-behaved friends.
(b) Everyone in the class – the more the merrier.
(c) Only my best friends – the ones who'll do what I tell them.
(d) A small number of friends – if you have too many, you only get a small slice of cake.
(e) Anyone noisy and naughty.

What sort of presents would you like to receive?

(a) I'd be grateful for anything – it's the thought that counts.
(b) Running shoes, stopwatch, sports gear.
(c) Give me something from my present list, or I'll scream.

(d) Sweets and chocolates.
(e) The latest robotic, electronic gadgets – anything that needs loads of batteries.

What sort of birthday tea would you like?

(a) Nice, healthy snacks like carrot and celery sticks.
(b) Lots of high energy food – but keep it quick – there won't be much time for eating.
(c) Whatever my favourite food is that week – if the others don't like it, it's tough.
(d) A slap-up, three-course meal.
(e) Chips, pizza, crisps, sweets and chocolate – yummy!

What kind of birthday cake would you like?

(a) Just a plain sponge – don't want any of my guests feeling sick.
(b) I'm not bothered about cake – just hand out some sweets, I can eat those on the go.
(c) I don't like cake, so my guests can't have any either.
(d) Any kind of cake is good – the bigger the better.
(e) The biggest gooiest chocolate cake ever!

Answers

Mostly (a)s: Just like Perfect Peter, you'd enjoy a traditional party at home with a small group of special friends. With games like 'Pin the Tail on the Donkey' and 'Pass the Parcel', and sandwiches, sausages on sticks and jelly for tea, everyone would have a jolly time.

Most (b)s: A big, beach party with loads of friends would really suit you – and Aerobic Al too. If you don't live anywhere near the sea, you could have it in a park instead. A picnic tea would leave lots of time for playing energetic team games, like rounders or cricket.

Mostly (c)s: A sleepover with two or three best friends would be the ideal party for you. Just like Moody Margaret, you like to be in charge, so at your party, what you say goes. You'd play a few games, listen to your CDs, and your friends would have to stay awake and listen to you talking all night!

Mostly (d)s: You'd enjoy a slap-up meal in a restaurant, with family and friends. Like Greedy Graham, the most important part of your party is the food! The highlight for you is always the great, big chocolate birthday cake.

Mostly (e)s: Like Horrid Henry, your idea of fun would be running around in dark tunnels, dressed as a spaceman, lazer-zapping your guests. You stuff your face with junk food, and create so much noise and mayhem that every year your parents groan, 'This is your last party ever.' (Until next year – tee hee!)

How to Make a Valentine's

Valentine's Day is a time to show someone you care about them – but not if you're Horrid Henry. Here's how Henry makes a joke Valentine's Day card to trick his arch enemy, Moody Margaret . . .

You will need:

2 pieces of card or paper, coloured or plain
Glue
Scissors
Pens, pencils or paint

Instructions:

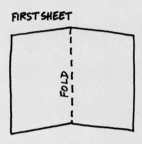

FIRST SHEET

FOLD

1. Fold one of the pieces of paper in half.

CUT

2. Work out roughly where the middle of the crease is, and cut a line about 5 cm long.

FOLD BACK

3. From the cut, fold back each of the flaps, as shown.

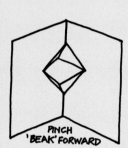

PINCH 'BEAK' FORWARD

4. Open up the card. Push one of the triangles up, and pinch the edges together hard, so that it is creased and looks a bit like a beak. Do the same with the other triangle.

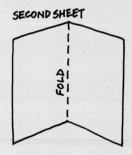

SECOND SHEET

FOLD

GLUE 1ST & 2ND SHEETS TOGETHER

DON'T GLUE BEHIND ★ 'BEAK' AREA! ★

5. Fold the second piece of card or paper in half. Glue this to the outside of the pop-up card. Try not to get any glue near the mouth or it won't open properly. When the glue is dry, draw a scary animal around the mouth.

DRAW SCARY FACE!

CUT ZIG-ZAG EDGE TO THE 'BEAK'!

6. Instead of a straight line, you could cut a zigzag line so it looks like scary teeth.

Card – Horrid Henry Style!

If you like, you can write a poem inside the card. Horrid Henry writes a rude one!

HAPPY VALENTINE'S DAY!

Roses are red
violets are blue
Moody Margaret
stinks
and so do
you!

From...
Guess Who?

NAH NAH NE
NAH NAH!!

29th February – it must be a Leap Year!

Every four years, it's a Leap Year, which means there's an extra day – the 29th February. Just imagine what it's like to be born on that day!

What will you do with your extra day?

Spring Sudokus

Can you fill in the coloured boxes so that each one contains an egg, a chick, a flower and a leaf? Don't forget – every row across and column down must contain all four pictures.

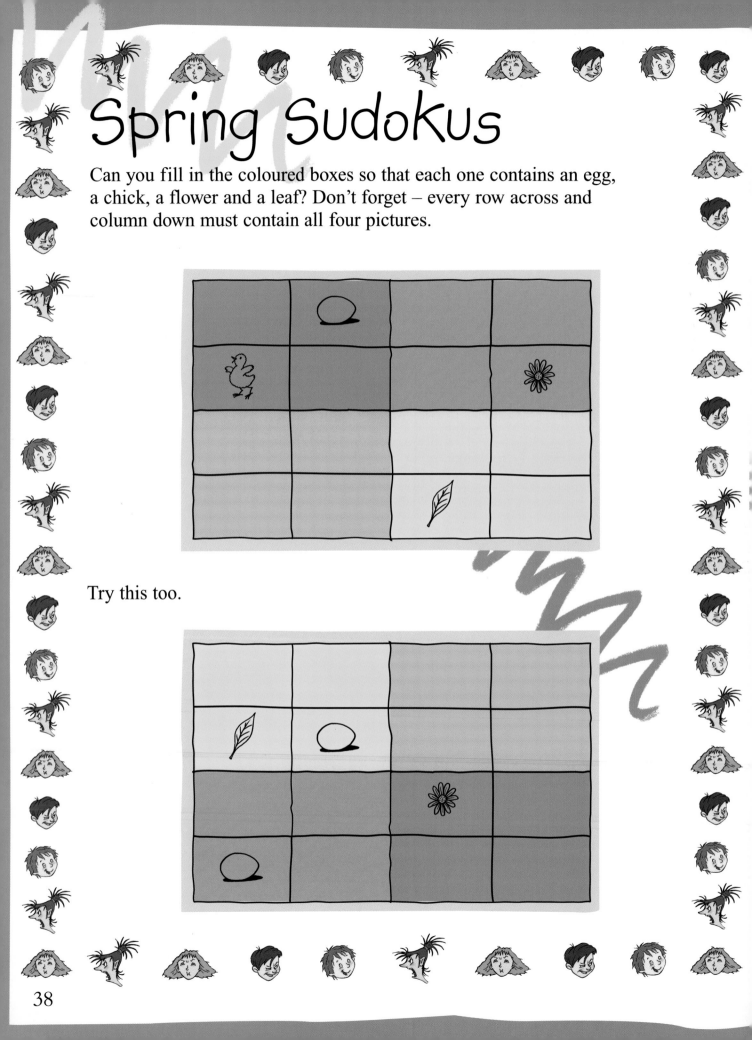

Try this too.

Mother's Day

MUM

Loves: Perfect Peter.
Hates: cooking.

Here's a frame for you to fill in.
You can draw a picture of your own
mum, or Horrid Henry's mum if
you prefer.

**What will you do
with your mum on
Mother's Day?**

_____

_____

_____

_____

_____

Easter Egg Hunt

It's Easter and Horrid Henry and Perfect Peter are having an Egg Hunt. There are five eggs hidden in Henry's room and five eggs hidden in Peter's room. Can you help Henry and Peter find them all?

Is your bedroom like Henry's or Peter's?

Are you an Egg Head?

How much do you really know about Horrid Henry? Try Brainy Brian's ten baffling brainbusters, and find out if you're a boffin or a buffoon.

1. **What is the name of the head teacher at Horrid Henry's school?**

   (a) Mrs Oddbod.
   (b) Mrs Oddbottom.
   (c) Mrs Codface.

2. **When Horrid Henry makes a stinkbomb to attack the Secret Club, he mixes two stinks together. Which two?**

   (a) Bad Breath and Nose Hairs.
   (b) Smelly Socks and Holey Vests.
   (c) Dead Fish and Rotten Egg.

3. **How does Henry trick Perfect Peter into handing over his Gold Gizmo?**

   (a) He tells Peter that two Green Gizmos are better than one Gold and offers to swap.
   (b) He tells Peter that every single person who has had a Gold Gizmo has died horribly.
   (c) He tells Peter that he'll be nice to him for ever.

4. **In the dance class show, is Henry . . .**

   (a) A banana?
   (b) A raindrop?
   (c) An elephant?

5. **Who lives next door to Horrid Henry?**

   (a) Moody Margaret.
   (b) Rude Ralph.
   (c) Sour Susan.

6. **When Henry goes camping with his family, what do they eat on their first night in camp?**

   (a) Spaghetti and meatballs.
   (b) Cold baked beans.
   (c) Pizza.

7. **How does Henry lose his first tooth?**

   (a) He bites into an apple.
   (b) He eats lots of sweets.
   (c) He ties string round the tooth, ties the string round a door handle – then slams the door!

8. **When Henry runs away from home, where does he go?**

   (a) Rich Aunt Ruby's house.
   (b) The Congo.
   (c) Moody Margaret's tree-house.

9. **What does Henry eat when the family go to Restaurant Le Posh?**

   (a) Snails.
   (b) Burger and chips.
   (c) Squid.

10. **When Henry sneaks a peek at Perfect Peter's diary, why is he so outraged?**

   (a) Peter writes horrible things about him.
   (b) Peter writes really nice things about him.
   (c) Peter doesn't write about him at all.

Turn to page 84 to see how many answers you got right, and find out whether or not you're as brainy as Brian!

7-10

Congratulations! You really are a brainy boffin. Make sure you read every new book about Horrid Henry and you'll stay at the top of the class.

4-6

Not bad – but not brilliant either. There's room for improvement, but you've got plenty of potential. Catch up on all the Horrid Henry books you've missed, and you'll soon be moving up to the top table!

1-3

Uh oh! Who's been reading all the wrong books?

Fun Fact Files: Foes

Miss Battle-Axe

Loves: History and giving loads of homework.

Hates: children.

Soggy Sid

Loves: chlorine.

Hates: dry land.

Can you draw pictures of your best and worst teachers in the picture frames?

Best Teacher

Worst Teacher

Horrid Henry's Perfect Pranks

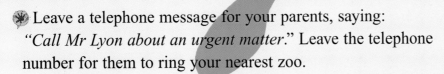

Horrid Henry loves April Fool's Day because he HAS to sneak around tricking people. Here are some of Henry's pranks – try them at your peril!

❋ Leave a telephone message for your parents, saying: "*Call Mr Lyon about an urgent matter.*" Leave the telephone number for them to ring your nearest zoo.

❋ Put salt in your hair, and tell your mum you've got dandruff.

❋ Make some silly stickers, saying things like '*I'm a Worm!*' or '*I love Miss Battle-Axe*' and stick them on people's backs.

❋ Make an April Fool's Day card for your parents. Write *Happy April Fool's Day* on the front, but stick all the edges together so that they can't open the card.

❋ At breakfast time, when no one is looking, swap your annoying brother's or sister's hardboiled egg for a raw one.

❋ Turn the clocks backwards or forwards so that everybody gets up far too early or far too late.

How to Make a Funny Fortune-Teller

Horrid Henry Gets Crafty

Even when it isn't April Fool's Day, Horrid Henry enjoys annoying people with his funny fortune-teller.

You will need:

A square piece of paper
Pens or pencils

Instructions:

 **1.** Find the middle of the paper by folding it from corner to corner.

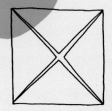 **2.** Fold each corner to the centre to make a smaller square.

 3. Turn the square over, and turn each corner to the centre again to make an even smaller square.

 4. Turn over again. Draw a different colour on each quarter of the square.

 5. Turn over again. Put numbers 1 – 8 on each segment.

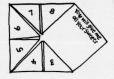 **6.** Open out each flap and write a message behind each number.

7. Put the thumb and forefinger of each hand into a segment and close up the fortune-teller. First ask your victim to choose a colour. If they choose RED, spell out R-E-D, and open and shut the fortune-teller three times. Then ask your victim to choose a number from the four numbers showing. Open and shut the fortune-teller however many times they choose. Then finally ask them to choose another number, open up the flap and read them the message.

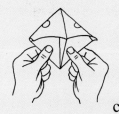

Fortunes

Horrid Henry's fortune-teller is full of horrible messages like…

- You're going to give me all your money.
- You will eat all my sprouts.
- You will give me all your sweets.
- You're going to marry Moody Margaret, nah nah ne nah nah.

Passover Puzzle

At school, Miss Battle-Axe teaches the class about the Jewish festival, Passover. It celebrates the time when God sent down the ten plagues and the Jewish people were freed from slavery in the land of Egypt. Even Henry likes learning about the ten plagues. Can you find them all in the wordsearch? Look forwards, backwards, down and diagonally.

The Ten Plagues

| Blood | Lice | Disease | Hail | Darkness |
| Frogs | Beasts | Boils | Locusts | Slaying |

B	O	I	L	S	L	B	C
E	L	O	C	U	S	T	S
S	Z	O	H	A	I	L	X
A	S	G	O	R	F	F	J
E	C	I	L	D	F	K	M
S	S	E	N	K	R	A	D
I	G	N	I	Y	A	L	S
D	B	E	A	S	T	S	N

Turn to page 84 to see how many plagues you found!

47

Pet Fact Files

FLUFFY

Loves: sleeping.

Hates: moving.

FANG

Loves: sunflower seeds.

Hates: Fluffy.

SHANTI (Francesca's dog)

Loves: having her tummy rubbed.

Hates: puddles.

How about drawing a picture of your own pet, or pasting in a photograph? If you don't have a pet, you could draw the pet you'd like to have.

If there are ten cats in a boat and one jumps out, how many are left?

None, they were all copycats.

Fun Fact Files: Friends

AEROBIC AL

Loves: running and winning lots of cups and medals.

Hates: sitting still.

Best Friend: Beefy Bert (easy to beat at all games).

WHEN I GROW UP I WANT TO BE:
an Olympic champion.

BRAINY BRIAN

Loves: puzzles and riddles no one else can solve.

Hates: questions I can't answer.

Best Friend: Clever Clare.

WHEN I GROW UP I WANT TO BE: an inventor.

CLEVER CLARE

Loves: hard maths problems.

Hates: getting answers wrong.

Best Friend: Brainy Brian.

WHEN I GROW UP I WANT TO BE: even smarter.

GORGEOUS GURINDER

Loves: mirrors.

Hates: the dark.

Best Friend: Lazy Linda.

WHEN I GROW UP I WANT TO BE: even more
gorgeous than I am now.

Horrid Henry's Homework

Horror of horrors! Miss Battle-Axe has given Henry homework. He has to write about 'MY MOST MEMORABLE MOMENT'. Here are four of Henry's finest moments.
Which one do you think he should choose?

'Horrid Henry and the Comfy Black Chair'.
Read the rest of the story in HORRID HENRY'S HAUNTED HOUSE.

Henry crept down the stairs and carefully opened the sitting room door. The room was pitch black. Better not turn on the light, thought Henry. He felt his way along the wall until

his fingers touched the back of the comfy black chair. He felt around the top. Ah, there was the remote. He'd sleep with that under his pillow, just to be safe.

He flung himself onto the chair and landed on something lumpy.

'AHHHHHHHHHH!' screamed Henry.

'AHHHHHHHHHH!' screamed the Lump.

'HELP!' screamed Henry and the Lump.

'Horrid Henry and the Demon Dinner Lady'.
Read the rest of the story in HORRID HENRY'S REVENGE.

Thump. Thump. Thump. The floor shook as the demon dinner lady started her food patrol. Horrid Henry waited until she was almost behind him. SNAP! He opened his lunchbox.

SNATCH! The familiar greasy hand shot out, grabbed Henry's biscuits and shovelled them into her mouth. Her terrible teeth began to chomp.

And then –

'Yiaowwww! Aarrrgh!' A terrible scream echoed through the packed lunch room.

Greasy Greta turned purple. Then pink. Then bright red.

'Horrid Henry's Haunted House'.
Read the rest of the story in HORRID HENRY'S HAUNTED HOUSE.

Some dreadful moaning thing was inside the wardrobe. Just waiting to get him. And then Horrid Henry remembered who he was. Leader of a pirate gang. Afraid of nothing (except injections).

I'll just get up and check inside that wardrobe, he thought. Am I a man or a mouse? Mouse! He thought. He did not move.

'Ooooooooaaaaahhhhhh,' moaned the THING. The unearthly noises were getting louder.

Shall I wait here for IT to get me, or shall I make a move first? thought Henry. Silently, he reached under the bed for his Goo-Shooter.

Then slowly, he swung his feet over the bed. Tiptoe. Tiptoe. Tiptoe.

Holding his breath, Horrid Henry stood outside the wardrobe.

'HAHAHAHAHAHAHAHA!'

Henry jumped. Then he flung open the door and fired.

SPLAT!

'Horrid Henry Goes to Work'.
Read the rest of the story in HORRID HENRY'S REVENGE.

Horrid Henry ran down the hall into Big Boss's office.

'Come quick, Bill's in trouble!' said Horrid Henry.

Big Boss dropped the phone and raced down the hall after Henry.

'Hold on, Bill, Daddy's coming!' he shrieked, and burst into the photocopy room.

There was Bossy Bill, perched on the photocopier, his back to the door, singing merrily:

'One bottom, two bottoms, three bottoms, four,

Five bottoms, six bottoms, seven bottoms, more!'

'Bill!' screamed Big Boss.

Father's Day

DAD

Loves: cooking.

Hates: Henry's music.

Here's a frame for you to fill in. You can draw a picture of your own dad, or Horrid Henry's dad if you prefer.

Creepy-Crawly Pizza

Horrid Henry loves pizza and hates having to share it with Perfect Peter. So Henry makes sure that Peter won't want even a bite – by creating his own terrible topping. Here's how.

You will need:

A pizza base
Chopped tomatoes, tinned tomatoes, tomato puree or passata sauce
Black olives
Red and yellow peppers
Cheese
Anchovies (if you like them)

Instructions:

1. Spread the pizza base with the tomato topping of your choice.

2. Sprinkle with grated cheese or lay on slices of mozzarella cheese.

3. Put black olives on top.

4. Cut the red and yellow peppers into thin slices and arrange them around the black olives so that they look like legs.

5. If you are using anchovies too, place them on the pizza, in squiggly shapes to look like creepy-crawlies.

6. Ask a grown-up to cook the pizza for you.

7. When the pizza is placed on the table, shout:

Gross-Out! Wiggly Worms!

Yuck! It's covered in blood!

Ugh! Creepy-Crawlies!

53

Horrid Henry's School Fair

It was the day of the school fair. Horrid Henry burst into the playground and went straight to the Treasure Map stall. There was the mystery prize, a large, tempting, Super Soaker-sized box. Wheee!

Cross Country Run

It's Sports Day and Horrid Henry, Perfect Peter and Aerobic Al are taking part in the Cross Country Run. But only one of them reaches the finishing post. Can you find out who it is?

FINISH

Miss Battle-Axe's School Report by Henry

Miss Battle-Axe's ~~Henry's~~ School Report

It has been horrible being tort by Miss Battle-Axe this year. She has shouted all day, and kept me in at

Behaviour: playtime for no reeson at all! She gives far too

English: much homework.

Maths: She has eyes in the back of her head, which makes

Science: copying other peeples work very difficult.

P.E:

She is the wurst teacher I have ever had. Miss Battle-Axe must try a lot harder, or else she will be in big trouble

Henry

Does your teacher deserve a good report or a bad one like Miss Battle-Axe? Fill in the report and write whatever you like. Just make sure your teacher doesn't see it!

Henry: I don't think I deserved zero on this test.

Miss Battle-Axe: I agree, but that's the lowest mark I could give you.

School Report

Behaviour:

English:

Maths:

Science:

P.E:

Horrid Henry's Top Parent-Taming Tips

- Never take 'no' for an answer.

- Don't forget to nag for what you want: eventually you will wear your parents down. If I can get Root-a-Toot trainers, anyone can.

- Tell your parents it's wasteful to have a TV and not to watch it.

- All computer games are educational. Remind your parents that you will never become a star fleet commander unless you get in lots of practice zapping enemy spaceships.

- Bedtime is for babies. Check out 'Horrid Henry's Bedtime' for the best ever schemes to postpone for hours that awful moment when you are in bed with the lights out.

- Shock your parents by doing something helpful every now and then without being asked. They will be so stunned and grateful that you can seize the moment and ask for more pocket money.

- Don't be *too* helpful, or you will spoil your parents. After all, they are your slaves and live to serve you.

  - Never leave getting presents to chance. Make sure you give your parents an up to date list of *everything* you want.

  - Remember, you're the boss.

Henry

Horrid Henry Goes Global

Horrid Henry is a hit all over the world, but he wouldn't always recognise his name. In France, he's called *Martin ZinZin*, in the Czech Republic, he's *Darebák David* and in Spain he's *Pablo Diablo*!

Can you spot Henry's name on these covers from around the world? See if you can pronounce them too! The answers are on page 84.

SKÚLI SKELFIR
(pronounced Esku
locskelvor)

RAMPETE ROBIN
(pronounced
Rahm-put Robin)

HÄIJY-HENRI
(pronounced
Ha-ee-ooh-Hen-ree)

HENRI HELYNT
(pronounced Henry
Hell-int)

RICO LA PESTE
(pronounced Reek-oh la pest-ay)

FELAKET HENRY
(pronounced Fel-are-ket
Henry)

Write Your Own Horrid Henry Story

Could you write a story about Horrid Henry? To give you a helping hand, Francesca has written a special story opening. All you have to do is finish it off! You can add some pictures, too.

Horrid Henry Goes to the Beach

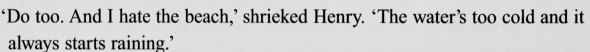

'No way! I'm not going and you can't make me!'

'Henry, we're going to the beach with Aunt Ruby and cousin Steve and that's that,' said Mum.

'But I hate Steve!' howled Horrid Henry.

'No you don't,' said Dad.

'Do too. And I hate the beach,' shrieked Henry. 'The water's too cold and it always starts raining.'

'I love the beach,' said Perfect Peter.

Horrid Henry attacked. He was a jellyfish stinging the flapping human to death.

'AAAeeeiiiiii!' squealed Peter.

'Don't be horrid, Henry!' shouted Mum.

'Get in the car,' shouted Dad. 'Everyone's waiting for you.'

Horrid Henry got in the car. He glared at Steve. Steve glared at him. Boy would they be sorry they'd made him come.

_____

_____

_____

_____

_____

The End

How to Run a Club

The long summer holidays are a great time to start your own club. Take a tip from these interviews with Horrid Henry and Moody Margaret to see how they run their rival clubs.

Horrid Henry

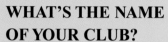

WHAT'S THE NAME OF YOUR CLUB?
The Purple Hand.

WHO'S THE LEADER?
Me – Lord High Excellent Majesty, of course.

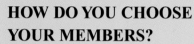

HOW DO YOU CHOOSE YOUR MEMBERS?
- The Leader always gets to choose the other members of the club.
- It's best to choose members who can bring lots of sweets and biscuits.
- Rude Ralph is a good member 'cause he burps a lot.
- I sometimes allow Peter to join in but only to keep guard – he'll never be a proper member 'cause he's smelly.

DO YOU HAVE A CLUBHOUSE?
Yes, it's my fort in the back garden and it has a throne for the Leader.

DO YOU HAVE A FLAG?
We have the Purple Hand Flag. I made it with an old pillow case and loads of purple paint. I dipped my hand in the paint and – SPLAT – the flag was finished.

WHAT PROVISIONS DO YOU HAVE?
Biscuits are best, especially if they are sneaked from the Secret Club biscuit tin, washed down with Fizzywizz drinks.

WHAT'S YOUR PASSWORD?
Smelly toads.

WHAT ARE THE CLUB'S MAIN ACTIVITIES?
- Raiding the Secret Club tree-house for biscuits.
- Attacking the Secret Club with stinkbombs.
- Spying on the Secret Club to discover their Master Plan.
- Setting booby traps to defeat the Secret Club.
- Swapping the Secret Club drinks for Dungeon Drinks.

Moody Margaret

**WHAT'S THE NAME OF
YOUR CLUB?**
The Secret Club.

WHO'S THE LEADER?
I'm in charge and everybody has to
do what I say.

**HOW DO YOU CHOOSE
YOUR MEMBERS?**
The Leader always chooses. Usually I choose
Sour Susan, but if she won't do what I say I
fire her and ask Lazy Linda instead. That
really makes Susan mad!

DO YOU HAVE A CLUBHOUSE?
My tree-house in the back garden.

DO YOU HAVE A FLAG?
Yes, it's a scary skull and crossbones.

**WHAT PROVISIONS
DO YOU HAVE?**
We have chocolate biscuits in the Secret Club
tin – unless the smelly boys from the Purple
Hand raid them all.

**WHAT'S YOUR
PASSWORD?**
It's Nunga – and I
respond with Nunga Nu. But I'll change it
straight away now.

**WHAT ARE THE CLUB'S
MAIN ACTIVITIES?**
- Keeping a spy report at all times.
- Despatching a spy to the enemy camp to
  report back on enemy activities.
- Recruiting and training a member of the
  Purple Hand to spy for us, by awarding
  him the Triple Star, the highest honour the
  Secret Club can bestow.
- Guarding the Secret Club biscuit tin.
- Attacking and raiding the Purple Hand
  Club camp.

Club Rules

All clubs need rules. Here are Horrid Henry's and Moody Margaret's very important rules.

The Purple Hand Rules

- Always obey the Leader.
- The Leader is to be called Lord High Excellent Majesty of the Purple Hand at all times.
- Always bring biscuits or sweets.
- You must say the password before you can enter the fort.

The Secret Club Rules

- Do what the Leader tells you. She's the boss.
- No one can enter without saying the password.
- Never ever tell the rival club the password.
- You can't quit if you've already been fired.

Now you can plan your very own club!

MY CLUB NAME _____

LEADER _____

MEMBERS _____

CLUBHOUSE _____

FLAG _____

PROVISIONS _____

PASSWORD _____

ACTIVITIES _____

RULES _____

Make a Wicked Waterbomb

Horrid Henry Gets Crafty

This waterbomb is fantastic for attacking a rival club. It's quite tricky to make at first, but it's easy once you know how.

You will need:

A square piece of paper
Water

Instructions:

1. Fold your square from corner to corner, to crease, as shown in the diagram.

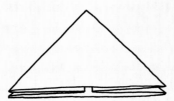

2. Push in the sides to create a triangle.

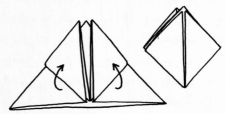

3. Fold up the corners to the point at the top. Turn over and repeat on the other side.

4. Fold in the sides. Turn over and repeat on the other side.

5. From the top, fold each of the flaps down and tuck into the sides, as shown. Turn over and repeat on the other side. Don't worry if they don't fit very neatly.

BLOW INTO HOLE

6. Gently pull your waterbomb into shape, then blow hard into the hole at the top.

FILL WITH WATER

7. Fill with water – and throw very quickly!

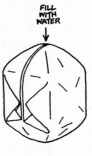

Secret Messages

All the best clubs have ways to pass secret messages between the members.

Here are a couple:

Invisible Ink

You will need:

Lemon Juice
A carrot with a pointed end
White paper

Instructions:

1. You'll be writing with the carrot so make sure it has a sharp point. If it doesn't, ask a grown-up to sharpen it for you.

2. Dip the point of the carrot in the lemon juice and write your message on the paper. Don't forget to keep dipping your carrot in the juice as you write.

3. Give your message to your club members. It will look like a blank piece of paper, until the paper is placed in direct sunlight or near a radiator. (The radiator must be on, as it's the heat that makes the message appear!)

Code Wheel

Every member of your club needs to have a Code Wheel.

You will need:

Paper or card
A butterfly-wing metal paper fastener
Pencils or pens

Instructions:

1. Trace around the large and small wheels and cut them out. Place the small circle on top of the large one, and attach in the middle with a paper fastener.

2. Start with the letter you'd like to put into code on the inner circle, matching its corresponding letter on the outer circle. Choose a magic number from 1 to 25. Move the inner circle clockwise that number of letters. Repeat this process for each letter in your message. For example, if you choose magic number 7, then A=H, B=I, C=J, and so on.

3. If you choose magic number 7, then to send a message to your club members, saying MEET AT THE FORT, you'd write TLLA HA AOL MVYA.

4. You also need to remember to write a small '7' on your note, so that the others know how to break the code.

67

Horrid Henry's Diary

Miss Battle-Axe said everyone had to keep a diary for a day. What a dumb, boring assignment! Why can't homework ever be playing computer games or watching TV? But no. I have to write about a day in my life. I already know how I spend my time! This is cruelty to children and I'm not writing a single word. I've got far too much else to do. So there. You can't make me. Ha ha ha.

Who cares if Mum and Dad find out I haven't done my homework and ban me from the computer for a month and take away my pocket money and unplug the TV and say 'no more crisps' . . .

Oh all right. I'll write it.

But *never* again.

8:00 am
The alarm goes off. I ignore it.
No way am I going to ~~she~~ school.

8:05
The alarm goes off again.
I ignore it.

8:06
Mum yells at me to get up.
I hide under the doovay

8:07
Dad yells at me to get up
I pretend it's a bad dream.

8:12
Peter comes in and says I'll be late for ~~sk~~ school if I don't get up. **Good** I say.

~~Nacher Nater Nat~~ Naturally, he's alreddy dressed.

<u>8:14</u>
Mum pulls the koovay off and screams at me to get up and get dressed **NOW**. ←Mum

I say I feel sick and I can't got to school. Mum doesn't believe me.

<u>8:15</u>
I heeve my heavy bones out of bed. I think makeing children get up at the crack off dawn to go to school is cruel and unusual punishment

<u>8.40</u>
Yikes! I can't find my school bag.

<u>8:44</u>
I find my school bag. What is it doing under the sofa?

<u>8:45</u>
Uh oh... I can't find my PE kit

<u>8:48</u>
I stil can't find my PE kit. Mum yells at me for not finding it.

<u>8:49</u>
I can't find my homework because I didn't do it. Oh well. Maybe Miss Battle-Axe will forget to ask us to hand it in.

Miss B-A

<u>8:50</u>
We leeve the house to walk to school. Dad asks me if I've brushed my teeth. Yes I say

<u>8:51</u>
I come back home to brush my teeth. We set out again.

<u>8:53</u>
Emergensy! I've forgotten my packed lunch. We rush back to get it.

<u>8:55</u>
Dad, Peter and I run like mad and get to school just as the final bell is ringing at 9:05

9:05 – 3:30
School. Work, work, work, work, work. Ugh. My best subject is lunch. I am brilliant at: eating, trading carrots for choclat and food fights. After lunch we do more work. I get into trouble for pokeing William, tripping Linda, shoving Dave, pinching Andrew, copying Clare, making rude noises, chewing gum, not doing my homework and talking in class. That's not so bad. In fact, that's prakticaly a perfect day. I bet I get mentioned in the Good as Gold Book!

3:30
~~School~~ School Ends. YiPPee!
4:00
I stretch out in the comfy black chair with a bag of crisps and switch on Rapper Zapper. BliSS.
4:12
Peter says it's his turn to watch Daffy and her Dancing Daisies. It's not fair!
4.22
Ralph phones. We make plans for tomorrow
4:45
I'm sent to my room for snatching the clicker and changing the channel to Mutant Max.

4:45 – 6:00
I read Comic books.
6:01
Dad yells at me to come down and lay the table. I don't here him. Well, I was busy.
6:10
I come downstairs very slowly and am to late too set the table. Boo hoo.
6:15 – 7:00
Dinner. I hate peas, so I flick them at Peter, and kick him. When he's not looking I snatch some of his chips Hmmm, boy! do those chips tast great!

Mum tells me of for chewing with my mouth open.

Dad tells me off for not using my fork.

Mum tells me of for Spitting

Dad tells me of for making a Mess

Mum tells me of for calling Peter an ugly toad and a Smelly nappy

They both tell me of for flicking peas at Peter and for kicking him. But I'm happy because Peter didn't notice I snatched his chips
Tee hee.

7:10 — 8:00
I screem and yell that I won't have a bath.

8:00 — 8:02
I have a bath

8:03
I tell Mum I don't have any homework. This may not be entirely true. But if I have homework I didn't write down what it was, and anyway I lost the worksheet Miss Battle-Axe may have handed out and there's no point in calling Ralph because he won't know about any homework so reely, I don't have any homework

8:04 — 8:15
I dance around my room singing along with the Driller Cannibals. I turn up the music as loud as I can. Mum and Dad scream at me to make it softer. I don't hear them - how could I? My music was loud! They burst into my room and turn of my tape. They are the meanest, most horrible parents in the world and I hate them.

Mum   Dad

8:16 — 8:25
I go into Peters room, and grab some of his toys. Then I sneek back into my room.

8:30
Peter says I've taken some of his toys. I tell him I haven't. Peter tells Mum. I get into trouble. BUT I will be revenged!

8:30 — 9:00
I red a fantastic book about a great kid who is always getting into trouble and who has a horrible younger brother who's perfect and two super mean parents. I can't remember the title but I reely recomend it.

9:00
Lights out. Time for my trusty flashlight to continue reading under the covers.

9:32
Mum confiscates my flash light. Just as well I have another one!

OOPS again

2:23 am

Yawn. Goodnight

Horrid Henry's Hike

Horrid Henry looked out of the window. It was a lovely day. Rats. Why couldn't it be raining? . . .
'Time to go for a walk,' called Mum.

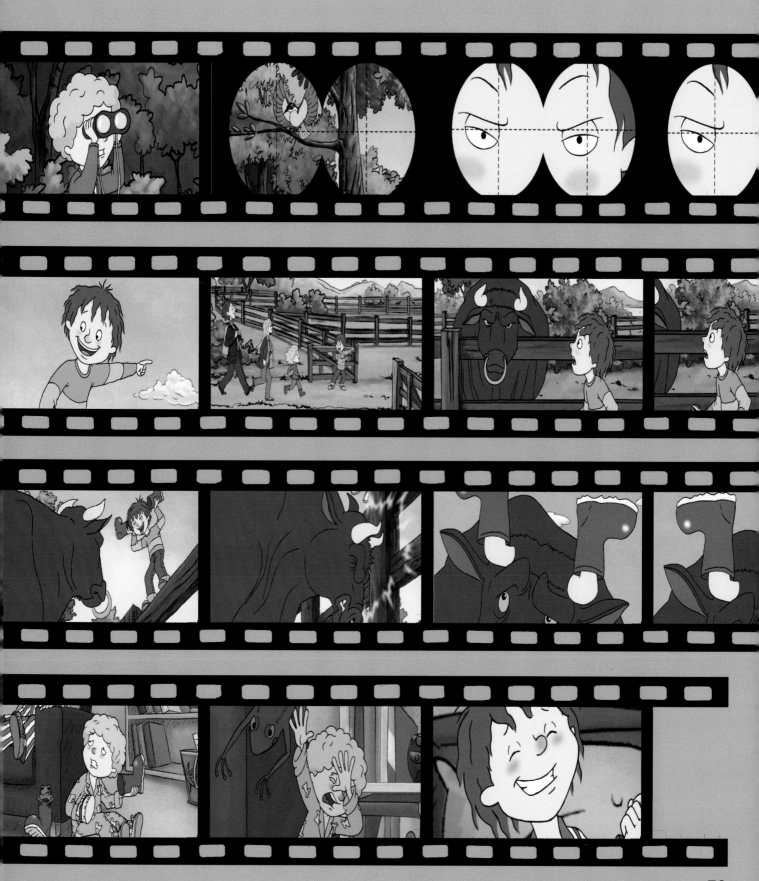

Halloween Happenings

WOOOOHOOOO! Here's how to be scary on Halloween – make a ghoulish ghost costume and a spooky spider.

Ghoulish Ghost

You will need:

An old white bed sheet
Tracing paper
Pencil
Black fabric paint

Instructions:

1. Trace the templates of the ghostly eyes, nose and mouth.

2. Cut out your tracings.

3. Try on the sheet and work out the best positions for the eyes, nose and mouth.

4. Draw around your tracings to transfer the eyes, nose and mouth onto the sheet.

5. Paint using the fabric paint.

6. Cut out eyeholes to make sure you can see where you're going!

7. If you can't use a sheet, you could make a ghost mask, using a pillowcase instead.

Spooky Spiders

You will need:

A lot of black wool   Scissors   Cardboard   Googly eyes (or you
A large-eyed needle   4 pipe-cleaners   Glue   can make your own
out of paper)

Instructions:

1. Cut out 2 cardboard circles, about 5½ cm in diameter, with a hole in the centre of each, about 2½ cm in diameter.

2. Thread the needle with the wool. Hold the 2 cardboard circles together and pass the needle through the centre hole and over the outside edge, over and over again until the circle is covered. Don't pull the wool tight.

3. When you have finished winding the wool, take the four pipe-cleaners and thread them through the hole in the centre of the cardboard. Bend them in the middle.

4. Now cut the wool between the edges of the two cardboard circles.

5. Double up a long length of wool. Slip it between the cardboard circles and tie it very tightly.

6. Carefully remove the cardboard circles.

7. Bend the spider's pipe-cleaner legs and stick on the eyes. Use the long piece of wool tied around the centre to hang the spider up in dark, gloomy corners.

Horrid Henry's Halloween Feel Box

Horrid Henry has a really horrible game for Halloween. If you want to make your friends and family scream and howl, follow Henry's instructions.

You will need a cardboard box – a large shoe box would be ideal. Cut a hole in the side of the box, large enough for a hand to fit through. Put a selection of grisly items into the box, and tell people to feel inside and guess what's there.

If you're having a Halloween party, sit in a circle in the dark and pass the items round one by one. Tell your guests that you are passing around a dead witch's brain, then hand round a damp sponge! Do the same for each of the items.

Here are a few ideas to get you started:

Dead witch's brains – damp sponge
Heart – hardboiled egg
Dried-up tongue – dried apricots
Veins – cold spaghetti
Eyeballs – peeled grapes or pearl onions
Skin – tortilla
Fingers – chipolatas
Nose – carrot
Ear – large mushroom

Sparkling Dot-to-Dot

With lots of noise and tons of toffee, Bonfire Night is Horrid Henry's idea of fun. Can you join the dots and find out what he's written with his sparkler in the sky?

Check your answer on page 84.

Christmas Criss-Cross

Can you fit all these Christmassy words into the criss-cross?
It's best to start with the longest word – CHRISTMAS!

9 Letters
CHRISTMAS

7 Letters
SNOWMAN

6 Letters
CAROLS
TINSEL

5 Letters
SANTA
ROBIN
HOLLY

4 Letters
STAR

3 Letters
IVY

Check your
answers on
page 84.

What goes Oh oh oh?
Santa walking
backwards

Horrid Henry's Christmas Presents

What I Want For Christmas:

TOP TEN Best Presents Ever

1. A million pounds.
2. Terminator Gladiator Game.
3. Super Soaker 2000: the best water blaster ever.
4. Intergalactic Robot Rebellion.
5. Intergalactic Samurai Gorillas, which launch real stinkbombs.
6. Deluxe Dungeon Drink.
7. Mega-Whirl Goo Shooter.
8. Ballistic Bazooka Boomerangs.
9. Robomatic Supersonic Space Howler Deluxe.
10. Zapatron Hip-Hop Dinosaur.

TOP TEN Worst Presents Ever

1. Walkie-Talkie-Teasy-Weasy-Burpy-Slurpy Doll.
2. Princess Pamper Parlour.
3. Baby Poopie Pants.
4. Big Girl Pants.
5. First Encyclopedia.
6. Scrabble.
7. Fountain pen.
8. Tapestry Kit.
9. Nature guide.
10. Lime green cardigan.

Can you list your TOP TENS?

1. _____
2. _____
3. _____
4. _____
5. _____
6. _____
7. _____
8. _____
9. _____
10. _____

Christmas Crackers

You will need:

2 loo rolls
Strong glue
Piece of crêpe paper – big enough to wrap around your cracker
Cracker 'bang' strip
Cracker goodies – eg: balloon, badge, stickers, sweets
Paper cut-outs – eg: snowman, holly leaves, Christmas tree

Instructions:

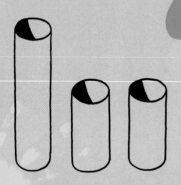

1. Cut 1 loo roll in half.

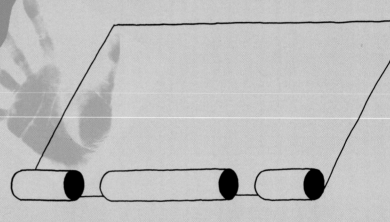

2. Using the crêpe paper sheet, stick the three cardboard rolls along one side, as illustrated.

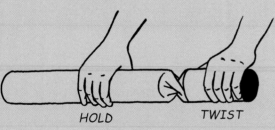

HOLD   TWIST

3. Holding the centre roll, carefully twist one of the end rolls.

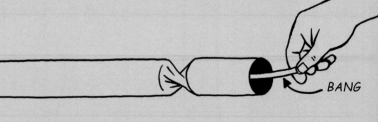

BANG

4. Insert cracker 'bang' strip through the twisted end.

GOODIES

5. Fill the cracker with goodies you'd like to have if you pulled a cracker!

6. Twist the other end of the tube, to contain the goodies.

7. Stick down both ends of the cracker 'bang' with glue.

BANG

GLUE BANG
BETWEEN CARD
AND PAPER AT
BOTH ENDS

8. Decorate the cracker with paper shapes you have drawn.

9. Pull the cracker with one of your friends!

When do astronauts eat?

At launch time.

What do you call babies' knees?

kid-neys

What do you get if you cross a cat with a tree?

A cat-a-log

Why are false teeth like stars?

Because they come out at night.

Horrid Henry's Top Ten Triumphs of the Year

1. Sneaked 865 sweets.
2. Did NOT do 15 pieces of homework.
3. Pinched Peter 250 times without Mum noticing.
4. Tricked Moody Margaret 100 times.
5. Tricked 3 Gold Gizmos off Peter.
6. Defeated the Demon Dinner Lady.
7. Was the best Innkeeper ever in the school Xmas play.
8. Persuaded Mum to buy me Root-A-Toot trainers.
9. Gave away all my nits.
10. Dropped ten million billion zillion peas on the floor.

Can you write down your own top ten triumphs?

1. _____
2. _____
3. _____
4. _____
5. _____
6. _____
7. _____
8. _____
9. _____
10. _____

See you
again soon!

Puzzle Answers

Page 38 Spring Sudokus

Page 40 Easter Egg Hunt

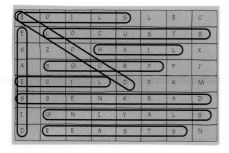

Page 42 Are you
an Egg Head?

1.(a); **2.**(c); **3.**(b); **4.**(b); **5.**(a);
6.(c); **7.**(a); **8.**(c); **9.**(a); **10.**(c);

Page 47 Passover Puzzle

Page 56 Cross Country Run

Henry is the only one to reach the
finishing post.

Page 59 Horrid Henry Goes Global

SKULI SKELFIR is published in Iceland.
RAMPETE ROBIN is published in Norway.
HAIJI HENRI is published in Finland.
FELAKET HENRY is published in Turkey.
RICO LA PESTE is published in Italy.
HENRI HELYNT is published in Wales.

Page 77 Sparkling Dot-to-Dot

Henry has written 'HENRY ROOLS'
with his sparkler.

Page 78 Christmas Criss-Cross

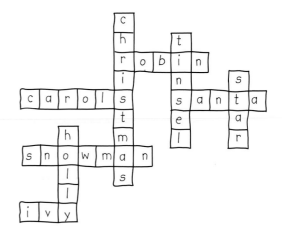

You can read these other *Horrid Henry* titles and all of them are
available as audio editions, read by Miranda Richardson

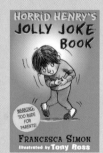

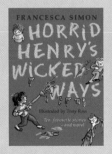

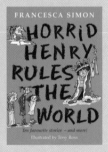

Horrid Henry is now a major animated television series
produced by Novel Entertainment Limited for CITV